MORE LETTERS FROM RUTH'S ATTIC

MORE LETTERS *from* RUTH'S ATTIC

31 DAILY INSIGHTS ON FOLLOWING CHRIST

RUTH BELL GRAHAM

Compiled from Decision *magazine*

BILLY GRAHAM EVANGELISTIC ASSOCIATION

Charlotte, North Carolina

All Scripture quotations, unless otherwise indicated, are taken from the Holy Bible, New International Version, NIV. © 1973, 1978, 1984, 2011 by Biblica, Inc. Used by permission of Zondervan. All rights reserved worldwide.

Scripture quotations marked NKJV are taken from the New King James Version. © 1982 by Thomas Nelson, Inc. Used by permission. All rights reserved.

Scripture quotations marked KJV are taken from the King James Version.

These devotions include edited excerpts from materials by Ruth Bell Graham previously published in *Decision* magazine. Used by permission.

ISBN: 978-1-59328-335-3

Foreword

My mother, Ruth Bell Graham, was a gifted author and poet. Although she's been in Heaven for a few years now, her writing still impacts people. She was a good storyteller with a unique perspective on life, not surprising since she had a rare and joyful attitude about everything from the whistling of the wind to a rainbow in the sky. She could put a smile on the weary face of a brokenhearted mother, she could brighten a darkened heart of someone running from God by speaking His truth, and she often prayed for—and with—many who had nearly lost the will to keep going. Today, the challenges and joys of life she wrote about still cause others to read her books and articles and contemplate her Lord and Savior Jesus Christ.

I believe you will find this true as you read through the pages of *More Letters from Ruth's Attic*. God bless you.

Franklin Graham
November 2011

v

Day 1

*It is good to praise the Lord and make music to your name,
O Most High, proclaiming your love in the morning and your
faithfulness at night.* —PSALM 92:1–2

Morning Song

Many years ago, I had been getting up early, fixing myself a cup of coffee and then sitting in the rocker on the front porch while I prayed for each of our children and for each of theirs.

One morning I awoke earlier than usual. It was 5 o'clock, with dawn just breaking over the mountains. I collected my cup of coffee and settled into the old rocker. Suddenly, I realized a symphony of bird song was literally surrounding me. The air was liquid with music, as if the whole creation were praising God at the beginning of a new day. I chuckled to hear the old turkey gobbler that had recently joined our family, gobbling away down in the woods at the top of his voice as if he were a song sparrow.

And I learned a lesson. I had been beginning my days with petitions, and I should have been beginning them with praise.

When the disciples asked our Lord to teach them how to pray, He gave them what we commonly know as the Lord's Prayer. The very first line is one of praise: "Hallowed be thy name."

In the 17th century, John Trapp wrote: "He lets out His mercies to us for the rent of our praise, and is content that we may have the benefit of them so He may have the glory."

Prayer for the Day:

Heavenly Father, I praise You for who You are and for the abundant blessings You provide. I join with all of creation in thanking You and worshiping You at the beginning of each day. To You be all the glory.

Day 2

Guide me in your truth and teach me, for you are God my Savior, and my hope is in you all day long. —PSALM 25:5

Pure Refreshment

It could be merely a piece of plywood stretched across two sawhorses, but you should have a special place for Bible study—a place that doesn't have to be shared with sewing, letter-writing or bill-paying. For years, mine was just an old wooden table between an upright chest of drawers and a taller desk.

On my desk I have collected a number of good translations of the Bible for reference, a Bible dictionary, a concordance and several devotional books. I also keep notebooks, a mug full of pens and a special pen that writes on the pages of my Bible without smearing or bleeding through.

When we were in school, we always kept a notebook handy to take notes on the professor's lecture. How much more important it is to take notes when God is teaching us!

If we have to clear off a spot for Bible study during a crowded day, we are likely to put it off. But if we have a place where our Bible is always open and handy, whenever there is a lull in the storm, we can grab a cup of coffee and sit down for a few minutes or more of pure refreshment and companionship.

Prayer for the Day:

In the midst of each day, Father, may I pause and allow Your Word to refresh and strengthen me. Let the Scriptures speak to me in a new and deeper way as I study and seek to understand what You are teaching me.

Day 3

Many are the plans in a person's heart, but it is the Lord's purpose that prevails. —PROVERBS 19:21

God Had Another Idea

Starting in childhood, I felt a strong tug toward serving God as a missionary in Tibet. It may have been a pipe dream—or, it could have been God checking out my willingness. No doubt the exposure to missionary speakers in chapel services at Wheaton College led me to the conclusion that I was called to be a missionary. And I planned to go alone. But God had another idea, and I married Billy Graham.

If I had insisted on having my way, I would have lasted in Tibet four years at the longest. Then that part of the world closed to foreign missionaries. And I would have missed the opportunity of a lifetime serving God with the finest man I know, having five terrific children and the most delightful grandchildren imaginable. All this, plus an unusual if not easy life.

I believe God had a part in my desire to go to Tibet. I think He was testing my willingness while at the same time preparing me for many long separations.

Mine has been the task of staying home and raising the family. No higher calling could have been given me. At the same time, it has been loads of fun. Also, I've had a vicarious thrill out of my husband's travels around the world in his unceasing attempt to carry the Good News to all who will listen.

Prayer for the Day:

Dear God, I know that Your plans for me are better than any plans I could make on my own. Make me sensitive to Your leading and willing to do what You call me to do.

Day 4

Do not be anxious about anything, but in every situation, by prayer and petition, with thanksgiving, present your requests to God. —PHILIPPIANS 4:6

It's Time to Pray

A good time for family prayers might be after the evening news on television. At this time, not only could we pray for our families and friends and local problems, but we could bring to the Lord the various crises and events portrayed on the screen.

If each evening, as the newscast concluded, a great wave of prayer across the world could ascend to God on behalf of those in trouble and those making trouble, what a difference it might make! We could pray by name not only for individuals involved, but also for each network newscaster and commentator. The greater the diameter of our knowledge of human needs, the larger will be the circumference of our petitions.

As J. Sidlow Baxter once said, "Men may spurn our

appeals, reject our message, oppose our arguments, despise our persons, but they are helpless against our prayers."

~

Prayer for the Day:

In the midst of my own prayer needs, dear Lord, help me to be sensitive to the needs of others. As I pray for events and those who bring the news to us, may my prayers join with those of many others around the world. Thank You for answered prayer.

Day 5

Look to the Lord and his strength; seek his face always.
—1 CHRONICLES 16:11

Feeling Trapped

The man, asleep in the trash bin, was awakened with a jolt. He had been scooped up with the trash by a 21-ton garbage truck. Knocked unconscious, he came to—upside-down and squeezed into an area where a human being shouldn't fit.

The truck started again and picked up two more loads of trash. When the driver stopped for a third load, he heard some hollering. Getting out, he looked around. The voice sounded far away, and he could see no one. So he started the compactor.

That's when he heard a banging inside the truck. Thinking something mechanical was wrong, he stopped the cylinders. Then, he later reported, he "heard a voice saying he sure would like to get out of wherever he was." Fortunately the driver saw to it that the man was freed.

That is the way I have felt at times: too much to do, too far to go, and not enough time or strength to do it all, so that I "sure would like to get out of wherever I am."

Someone has said, "God does not promise strength for uncommanded work." Perhaps you're attempting things He hasn't commanded. When I began to feel compacted and cried for help, God showed me how my priorities had gotten distorted. He was to come first. Then I realized that I needed to be liberated from wherever I was. I needed to get off of boards and committees, write no more books or articles for the time being, and accept fewer outside responsibilities. This was God's answer for me. He has a solution for you as well.

Prayer for the Day:

Dear God, I want to seek You and Your will for my life above all else. Guide me to the work You want me to do, and give me Your strength to accomplish it.

Day 6

I call on you, my God, for you will answer me; turn your ear to me and hear my prayer. —PSALM 17:6

Power in Prayer

The center of power, it has been said, is not found in summit meetings or in peace conferences. It is found when children of God pray for God's will to be done in their lives, in their homes and in the world around them.

We cannot pray and remain the same. We cannot pray and have our homes remain the same. We cannot pray and have the world around us remain the same. God has decreed to act in response to prayer. He commands us to ask. And Satan trembles for fear we will.

When we were growing up in China, bandits kidnapped the two children of our hospital business manager. The bandits held the children for ransom, but it was against mission policy to pay ransoms.

Everyone—missionaries, Chinese friends, co-workers, even we children—prayed. In a few weeks the children were returned—without ransom—a thing unheard of in China at the time.

When I was a child, there was a man named Ma Er who helped our family. The man had gone AWOL from the Chinese army, which found him and cut off his ears. Ma Er was not a Christian. When I left China to go to boarding school in North Korea, Ma Er's name was on my prayer list. Years later I learned that my prayers had been answered—Ma Er had given his heart to the Lord Jesus and had become a sincere believer.

Be pointed. Be persistent. Be patient. But pray.

Prayer for the Day:

When I pray, Father, I know that You hear me. Plant in me the ability to be patient yet persistent in prayer. May Your will be done in my life, my home and my world.

Day 7

Many will see and fear the Lord and put their trust in him.
—PSALM 40:3

Offering Christ

Pashi was a student in our local college. He was from India, and when presented with the claims of Christ, Pashi's devastating reply was: "I would like to believe in Christ. We of India would like to believe in Christ. But we have never seen a Christian who was like Christ."

Come to think of it, neither have I.

We believers are all merely pilgrims in progress, encumbered with disagreeable genes, trying—and in the process being found "trying indeed." The very term *Christlike* is confusing. In what way are we to be like Him? In His ability to heal, to teach, to cast out demons? To face His accusers silently?

I think the term has to do with Christ's attitude toward His Father's will.

"*I delight to do thy will*" (Psalm 40:8, KJV).

Whatever the true meaning, I was feeling we Christians had let the Lord down. I decided to call our co-worker and friend, Dr. Akbar Haqq, a brilliant Christian who once was president of the Henry Martyn School of Islamic Studies in New Delhi.

"How would you answer Pashi?" I asked him.

"I would tell him, 'I'm not offering you Christians,'" Akbar answered decisively. "'I am offering you Christ.'"

❧

Prayer for the Day:

Lord Jesus, I want to be like You in all that I do, but I also want to remember that it is You people need, not my weak imitation of You. Help those I know to see and receive You in spite of me.

Day 8

In his love and mercy he redeemed them; he lifted them up and carried them all the days of old. —ISAIAH 63:9

Our Father Carries Us

The young father walking on the beach lifted up his son to sit on his shoulders. Each leg firmly held in his father's hands, the boy sat happily. He had a view that he otherwise could not have enjoyed.

And he was safe—safe from the blistering hot sand on the beach, the onrushing waves, the sharp shells or broken glass in the sand. He could go indefinitely without becoming tired. Sitting on his father's broad shoulders, he wouldn't have to run to keep up ... it would be no problem.

As I watched them, I thought of Moses, who told the children of Israel: *"The Lord your God carried you, as a man carries his son"* (Deuteronomy 1:31, NKJV). And God assures us, *"Even to your old age, I am He, and even to gray hairs I will carry you! I have made, and I will bear; even I will carry, and will deliver you*" (Isaiah 46:4, NKJV).

Being lifted up and carried securely is not just for little boys on beaches; it also is for those of old age, those with gray hair.

Seeing the father on the beach reminded me that there is One who lifts us up and carries us. He is our Heavenly Father Himself.

⤙⤚

Prayer for the Day:

Lord, I am grateful that You have carried me through past trials. Thank You for Your assurance that You lift me up and carry me in all situations.

Day 9

Therefore, as we have opportunity, let us do good to all people, especially to those who belong to the family of believers.
—GALATIANS 6:10

Falling Flat on One's Face

Who among us hasn't, at one time or another, fallen flat on our face? Some people seem more prone to fall than others, more prone to failure.

I recall one baby Christian (a grown man, but a baby Christian) who, if I believed in reincarnation, I would have said was the Apostle Peter back again—hot-tempered, big-hearted and impulsive.

The older Christians were waiting for this man to fall, and it wasn't long before he obliged them.

He said later that the greatest stumbling block in the beginning of his Christian life was not his old drinking buddies, but skeptical Christians waiting for him to fall flat on his face so they could say, "I told you so!"

Many of us feel we have the gift of discernment when it comes to the faults and failures of other Christians—and on top of that, the gift of disapproval as well. But even our Lord came not to condemn (we were already condemned), *"but that the world through him might be saved"* (John 3:17, KJV).

"If a brother be overtaken in a fault [a different way of saying 'falling flat on one's face,' perhaps] you who are spiritual restore such a one" (cf. Galatians 6:1).

Who in your family or among your acquaintances do you most heartily disapprove of? Don't you think that one is already eaten up with guilt? How can you show them kindness?

Prayer for the Day:

Sometimes I am guilty of finding fault instead of seeking to restore a fellow Christian. Jesus, give me Your wisdom to lift up my brother or sister in love.

Day 10

"I Didn't Do It!"

It was near suppertime, and my instructions were clear: "No watermelon!"

Soon after, I discovered watermelon juice punctuated with seeds all over the stone steps. I summoned the likely young culprit.

"I didn't do it!" he said flatly.

"You must have," I replied, pointing to the mess.

"No."

"Come with me," I said. In his bedroom I said, "Listen, God knows exactly what happened."

"Aw, Mom," the small voice interrupted. "Him doesn't know. Him's just guessing!"

I replied firmly, "He saw. Let's pray, and you tell God you are sorry that you disobeyed and lied about it."

19

Now, thinking about this situation, I have concluded that we are like escape artists in not wanting to accept responsibility for our actions.

The old Episcopal Prayer Book includes this confession: "I have sinned ... by my fault, by my own fault, by my own most grievous fault."*

Perhaps we need to face the fact that reasons are not excuses and lies are not acceptable. While we may not be responsible for what happens to us, we are responsible for how we react to circumstances. And we all are ultimately responsible to God.

Prayer for the Day:

Dear God, I am not always willing to admit my sins, but You know anyway. Give me the courage to confess when I disobey You and to seek forgiveness from anyone whom I might have hurt. Thank You for Your mercy.

*In *Saint Augustine's Prayer Book: A Book of Devotion for Members of the Episcopal Church*, revised edition, edited by Loren Gavitt, Holy Cross Publications, New York, New York, 1947, 1967

Day 11

And the God of all grace, who called you to his eternal glory in Christ, after you have suffered a little while, will himself restore you and make you strong, firm and steadfast.
—1 PETER 5:10

Salvaged, and Restored

He had built for himself a great house that was a thing to behold. It was a masterpiece of salvaged materials.

He collected and sold scrap metal as well as antiques, and he was fascinated with broken bits and pieces of china dug from his front yard. Carefully he fitted and glued the pieces together. Few objects ever came out whole. They were simply the collection of one who cared.

I expressed an interest in his work, and he gave me a blue-and-white plate that had been carefully glued together, despite pieces that were missing.

I commented, "You remind me of God."

I knew from the look on his face that I had shocked him, and I hurried to explain: "God takes our broken lives and lovingly pieces them together again. Even if a piece has been lost, God gathers what He can and restores us to wholeness in Him."

~∙~

Prayer for the Day:

When I make a mess of my life, Lord, salvage the broken pieces and restore me to wholeness. Create something new and beautiful that reflects Your love to all who know me.

Day 12

Jesus looked at them and said, "With man this is impossible, but not with God; all things are possible with God."
—MARK 10:27

Incompatible?

It happens all the time: Well-known couples terminate marriages. The reason? Incompatibility. It's an all too familiar legal umbrella under which an assortment of excuses finds shelter.

I looked up the definition of "incompatibility": *incapable of coexisting harmoniously ...*

Incapable of coexisting harmoniously? "With God, all things are possible," I remembered.

The definition continued: *disagreeing in nature.* Great! One can disagree without being disagreeable. Before we married, someone gave me a gem of wisdom: "Where two people agree on everything, one of them is unnecessary."

Irreconcilable. I doubt it! When two draw near to God,

they find themselves closer to one another.

Conflicting. Terrific! When someone gets into a position of political or social power or one of fame or fortune and no one dares to disagree with him or her, look out! This person is in danger. At times, we all need to be disagreed with.

Our daughter's Swiss in-laws once gave my husband a Swiss watch. Eventually, it stopped working, but no local watchmaker could fix it. The next time we were in Switzerland, we sent it directly to the company that made it. They had no problem; the ones who made it knew how to make it work again.

Who invented marriage? He is the One to whom we must go. His Book of Instructions has the answers.

———

Prayer for the Day:

God, whether it is marital difficulties, family or work relationships, or a broken friendship, Your Word provides the answer. Thank You for Your promise that all things are possible when I trust You.

Day 13

When Our Instructor Speaks

They splashed and they flopped, those aspiring wind surfers. Day after day we chronicled their struggles. It looked simple enough: a surfboard, a detachable sail with a length of rope tied to it, water, wind and, of course, instruction.

But the sail would go flat on the water, with the surfer splashing into the water on the other side. Or the surfer would jump into the water to avoid being clobbered by the mast. Then the surfer would struggle to board again, try to balance, try to pull the sail back to position—then plop!

The next summer a few surfers had more or less mastered the art of windsurfing. With surprising skill, they skimmed around on the water even on rough days. We watched surfers aid a fallen surfer;

25

we heard them shout encouragement to one another.

One person could maneuver his craft wherever he wanted it to go. He was, we later discovered, the instructor.

When the instructor spoke, they listened and tried to do what he said. Windsurfing is a skill to master through unending patience and dogged determination.

Like windsurfing, living the Christian life looks simple, but it is not easy. Someone has said that the perseverance of the saints consists in ever new beginnings. So we who are mature in the Christian walk need to be quick to help the one who has fallen, and quick to encourage one another.

We all need to work at mastering the art of Christian living and to study our Book of Instructions. We all need to listen attentively when our Instructor speaks and promptly follow His instructions.

Prayer for the Day:

Give me patience and perseverance as I try to follow You, Jesus. Through Your Word, remind me daily of Your instructions for life and teach me how to encourage others.

Day 14

This is how we know what love is: Jesus Christ laid down his life for us. And we ought to lay down our lives for our brothers and sisters. —1 JOHN 3:16

"The One I Missed"

It was December 1958. A tragic fire at a parochial school in Chicago, Ill., was being reported on the evening news, and one of the teachers was being interviewed. She told of the panic among the children, the suffocating heat and the smoke that blackened the room in daylight. And she told of helping the children out the window and down the ladders, assisted by the firefighters.

Struggling for control, the teacher described how she had climbed through the window and down the ladder, across the roof and down another ladder to the ground.

"I looked up at the windows and the billowing black smoke," she said. With tears streaming down her face, she continued, "It was then that I saw the one I missed."

Amid the pressures of today, the increasing global turmoil—the smoke that blackens the room in daylight—we who are Christians must be alert to the needs of others. Is there a letter that we could write? A simple deed of kindness that we should do? An encouraging word to give to someone who is desperate to hear? Time that we ought to take to listen? Is there someone we should invite for a meal or a cup of tea?

We need to be concerned. We need to have compassion. This is not the same as telling others of the Gospel. Opportunities to help others allow us to show genuine love, to earn the right to be heard, so that we can tell them about Jesus Christ. God forbid that the time should ever come when we will have to look back and see "the one we missed."

Prayer for the Day:

Father, never let me live with regret for the one I missed. Show me each day the ways that I can meet the needs of others, so that I can tell them about Your Son who died because of Your great love for them.

Day 15

We were under great pressure, far beyond our ability to endure, so that we despaired of life itself. Indeed, we felt we had received the sentence of death. But this happened that we might not rely on ourselves but on God, who raises the dead. He has delivered us from such a deadly peril, and he will deliver us again. On him we have set our hope that he will continue to deliver us.
—2 CORINTHIANS 1:8–10

Capstones, Not Compactors

There are different kinds of pressures. I want to talk about necessary, even creative, pressure—not pressure that destroys and debilitates. Capstones, not compactors.

Have you ever studied an old stone arch? The capstone supports the weight of the whole; it bears the pressure.

We appreciate the value of pressure when we see a tourniquet applied, thus stopping the flow of blood and saving a life.

J. Hudson Taylor, the great pioneer missionary to China,

29

used to say we should not mind how great the pressure is—only where the pressure lies. If we make sure it never comes between us and our Lord, then the greater the pressure, the more it presses us to Him.

Perhaps our secret of "grace under pressure" lies in accepting that pressure as from the Lord, or at least permitted by Him.

It may be one more request than we think we can fulfill, one more responsibility than we think we can manage, one more phone call, one more pile of dishes to wash, one more bed to make, one more room to clean, one more complaint to listen to, one more interruption ...

Yet, as we accept it as from Him, asking Him to teach us what He would have us learn through the experience, as we use it for the good of others and for His glory, pressure will have fulfilled its purpose.

~

Prayer for the Day:

When circumstances press in on me, Jesus, give me grace. Teach me what You want me to learn from the experience, and press me closer to You.

Day 16

Trust in the Lord forever, for the Lord, the Lord himself, is the Rock eternal. —ISAIAH 26:4

Look to the Rock

Several years ago my brother and sisters and I were completing a pilgrimage to our old home in China. I had asked permission to call on two well-known, elderly Christians. They had served a combined total of 37 years in hard-labor camps because of their Christian faith.

When I went to visit them, though, they were away from home. Disappointed, I was complaining to the Lord on my way back to the hotel. I felt that I needed to visit these two people—to learn of the all-sufficiency of our God and how He had met their needs.

Suddenly, seemingly from nowhere, came these words: *"Look unto the rock whence ye are hewn"* (Isaiah 51:1, KJV).

I had not consciously memorized this verse of Scripture. At the time I did not even know where in the Bible it was found. But God used those words to remind me that I was not to look to people but to Him. He meets each individual according to his or her particular need, and according to His graciousness. Furthermore, God might not meet my need in just the same way that He had met theirs. But He would meet it.

Later, when I did visit this dear couple, I found them to be full of gratitude to God for His goodness and His faithfulness. They felt no bitterness; they were loving and happy.

And I was doubly blessed: first in the missing when I learned to look to the Rock, and then in the meeting when I learned of God's all-sufficiency.

———✦———

Prayer for the Day:

I praise You, God, for meeting my needs in Your goodness and in Your timing. Help me to trust You when I would rather complain. Turn my eyes always to You, the Rock of my salvation.

Day 17

And you are complete in Him, who is the head of all principality and power. —COLOSSIANS 2:10, NKJV

Scaffolding

The famous Gate of Heavenly Peace, in Beijing, China, was shrouded in bamboo scaffolding. It was showing the wear of time and the brutalizing of wars and revolts, along with the ravages of pollution, so necessary restoration was now under way.

It was 1980 and I was in China with my two sisters and my brother as part of a pilgrimage to our old home. After China, my older sister and I boarded an airplane for Greece.

In Athens, the Parthenon was covered with scaffolding. What weather and wars had failed to do in 2,500 years, pollution had accomplished in just a few.

Our next stop was France. After 40 years of construction, the Palace of Versailles was completed in about 1710. The royal chapel was added later—the chapel was now covered with scaffolding.

We drove to Chartres to see the Cathedral of Notre Dame, one of the finest examples of Gothic architecture. Once more we found scaffolding.

From France we flew to England, where we visited Westminster Abbey. As we approached the Abbey, so alive with history, what did we see? You've already guessed—scaffolding.

Is that the way the world sees the church?

The church is scarred by wars, buffeted by storms and eroded by pollution, and God is at work restoring His own—repairing, cleaning, purifying. He sees the end from the beginning. He sees us "complete in Christ" (cf. Colossians 2:10), and the day will come when *we shall be like him*" (1 John 3:2, KJV).

But in the meantime, the world sees mainly the scaffolding.

❧

Prayer for the Day:

Lord, when I am battered and scarred, do Your reconstruction work in me. Repair me, cleanse me, purify me. Through my life, show Yourself to others around me.

Day 18

Your word is a lamp for my feet, a light on my path.
—PSALM 119:105

Collectibles

People are writing and talking about "collectibles." They can be a hedge against inflation, sort of a cushion in case of a depression. They are small items that initially may cost little or nothing but that increase startlingly in value in a relatively short period of time. Included are old stamps, rare coins, old photographs, paintings, even certain cans and bottles.

I got to thinking. What would be the best collectible for me? Something that would increase in value; something that would make me really wealthy; something I could share that would be a cushion in case of depression and could provide comfort in case of the death of a loved one or old age.

I had it! Bible verses. I had started long ago.

In China, Miss Lucy Fletcher offered us, her students,

$5 (a lot of money for a missionary's kid) if we would memorize the Sermon on the Mount. Hours and hours of going over and over Matthew 5, 6, 7. When the time came to recite it, I made one mistake and so I got only $4.50. But I wouldn't take a thousand times that amount in place of having memorized it.

Prayer for the Day:

Lord, thank You for giving me the treasure of Your Word. Help me to share Scriptures that will show others Your light in times of darkness.

Day 19

Have mercy on me, O God, according to your unfailing love;
according to your great compassion blot out my transgressions.
Wash away all my iniquity and cleanse me from my sin.
—PSALM 51:1–2

Clogged Pens

I shook it. I knocked it gently, sideways on the top of the desk. I licked a piece of paper and wrote carefully in the moisture—I can't tell you why this works, but it usually does. I repeated each procedure without results. Then I carried the pen to the sink, took it apart and carefully flushed out the point. Refilling it, I sat down to write.

How like me, I thought with exasperation.

I have mugs full of pens on my desk: ballpoints, felt tips, ink pens—even pencils. But for very fine writing, such as notes in the margin of my Bible, I need a Rapidograph pen. This pen has a needle-fine point and uses India ink, which will not soak through or smear on the thin India paper.

How often when God has needed me I have been clogged up—too busy or inundated with things, the necessary giving way to the unnecessary. Or I've gone dry.

When that happens, I need a shaking up or a special cleansing. And I need to be filled and refilled and filled again.

There have been times when God has patiently and carefully done just that. There have been other times when He has had to pass me over and pick up a pen that was usable.

But unlike a pen, I have a choice. I can decide whether or not I remain usable.

Prayer for the Day:

Lord, I want to be usable in Your hands. When necessary, shake me up, wash me and fill me again, so that I remain ready when You ask.

Day 20

You are the salt of the earth. But if the salt loses its saltiness, how can it be made salty again? It is no longer good for anything, except to be thrown out and trampled underfoot.
—MATTHEW 5:13

Do We Make People "Thirsty"?

In a country whose leaders denied the existence of God but allowed the church to exist under a secretary for church affairs, the secretary was not only a pastor but a medical doctor as well.

One day he was called before the authorities. Knowing that there would be a new crackdown on Christians, he said, "I know you wish to interrogate me, but, first, may I say something?"

Permission granted, the doctor continued, "You know that I am a medical doctor. I know the importance of salt in the human body: It needs to be about 2 percent of the body weight. If it becomes less or is absent, a person may become ill or even die.

"Jesus Christ said that Christians are the 'salt of the earth.'" Then the doctor paused. "That is all. And now, gentlemen, what is it that you wish to say to me?"

"Oh, nothing, nothing," they answered and dismissed him.

In Numbers 18:19 the Bible refers to a *covenant of salt*." The Greeks have a saying, "Trespass not against the salt and the board." An Arab saying goes, "There is salt between us." A modern Persian phrase is "untrue to salt," which means to be disloyal or ungrateful.

Salt is indispensable to the health of people and of livestock. Salt also is a preservative and a seasoning, as well as brine in refrigeration.

But another fact about salt is that salt makes a person thirsty.

Do we Christians, as the "salt of the earth," make people thirsty for the Water of Life?

—◆—

Prayer for the Day:

Give me a thirst for You, dear Jesus. Help me to live in a way that others will ask for the Water of Life that only You can provide.

Day 21

God is not human, that he should lie, not a human being, that he should change his mind. Does he speak and then not act? Does he promise and not fulfill? —NUMBERS 23:19

Asking God "Why?"

Sometimes the question *Why?* is wrenched from a person—even from earnest believers.

While I was growing up in China, one of our fellow missionaries committed suicide. Overworked and under unbearable pressure, this dear Christian broke.

Left untended for a brief moment, a child of missionaries fell into a tub of scalding water. Not long after that, the daughter of those same missionaries died after eating poisonous beans.

Sometime later a missionary friend was shot and then beheaded by bandits. When I was in high school in Korea, a fellow student was killed by a train. His death affected the entire student body.

From time to time throughout our lives, our cry of

anguish goes up to God: "Lord God, take away our pain."

But still, pain—unexpected, unendurable, unexplained—continues to strike us.

Is it wrong for us to ask, "Why?"

When Moses asked, "Why?" God's answer was, *"Now you will see what I will do"* (Exodus 6:1).

Even our Lord Jesus once asked "Why?"—on the cross at Calvary.

Someone has said that faith never asks why. But surely, involuntarily, one must often cry out, "Why?"

We need to pray for courage to ask the right questions so that we will be prepared for the answers.

❧

Prayer for the Day:

Dear God, I am grateful for Your faithfulness. When life doesn't make sense, give me grace to understand and patience to endure. Help me to seek Your answers to the difficult questions that I have.

I eagerly expect and hope that I will in no way be ashamed, but will have sufficient courage so that now as always Christ will be exalted in my body, whether by life or by death.
—PHILIPPIANS 1:20

Afraid? Of What?

Living in China in an area where kidnapping for ransom was not uncommon, what did one do? Wealth is comparative, but to the Chinese bandit of that day, the average foreigner appeared wealthy. Our mission board made it a policy never to pay ransom, a policy that spread rapidly by word of mouth. As a result, none of our missionaries was ever held for ransom. One, however, was killed in cold blood.

"Uncle" Jack Vinson* was recovering from an appendectomy when bandits pillaged a village inhabited by a number of Christians. He insisted on going to check on them. While he was there, the bandits returned and Uncle Jack was captured. After being roped together with a long line of prisoners, he was ordered to start walking.

Because of his recent surgery, he was unable to keep up.

A young Chinese girl heard a bandit threaten to shoot him if he did not hurry. Uncle Jack replied, "If you shoot me, I shall go straight to Heaven." The soldier shot him.

When "Uncle Ham" heard this account, he wrote a poem that I think reflects the feelings of all those missionaries under whose influence we were reared.

Afraid? Of What?
To feel the spirit's glad release?
To pass from pain to perfect peace,
The strife and strain of life to cease?
Afraid—of that?

Afraid? Of What?
Afraid to see the Savior's face
To hear His welcome, and to trace
The glory gleam from wounds of grace?
Afraid—of that?

Afraid? Of What?
A flash, a crash, a pierced heart;
Darkness, light, O Heaven's art!
A wound of His a counterpart!
Afraid—of that?

44

Afraid? Of What?
To enter into Heaven's rest,
And yet to serve the Master blest,
From service good to service best?
Afraid—of that?

Afraid? Of What?
To do by death what life could not—
Baptize with blood a stony plot,
Till souls shall blossom from the spot?
Afraid—of that?
　　　—E.H. HAMILTON

Prayer for the Day:

Lord, help me to boldly face trials, even death, with confidence in Your promise of eternal life. Thank You for conquering death and giving me hope in place of fear.

*The children of missionaries often called fellow missionaries "aunt," "uncle" or "cousin."

Day 23

And we know that in all things God works for the good of those who love him, who have been called according to his purpose.
—ROMANS 8:28

Harvest From Tragedy

In 1900 the Boxer Rebellion erupted in China. Westerners gathered in Shanghai, Peking and provincial capitals to seek asylum. There were daily reports of missionaries and faithful Chinese Christians brutally murdered by the Boxers.

Then came the blackest day of all. Between 46 and 100 missionaries had sought refuge in the courtyard of the Shansi governor, not knowing he was a leader in the Boxer uprising. All were executed.

The question "Why?" trembled on the lips of more than one missionary. The need had been so great, and now this waste.

In the grim stillness following, one missionary returned to his home 300 miles north.

Soon, a stranger visited him. The stranger, with his hard face and authoritative bearing, asked, "Do you remember the foreigners who sought protection from the governor of Shansi Province?"

"I have heard."

The stranger sat silent a few minutes, then said, "I am captain of the bodyguard. I was in charge."

"You were responsible?" The missionary could have lashed out at the captain. But something in the captain's face stopped him.

The captain continued, "To me, it was nothing. I am accustomed to killing. The governor does not like foreigners. When they gathered at his door asking for protection, he replied, 'I can protect you only by putting you in the prison.'

"So he put them in prison. For several days his hatred grew. Then he gave me my orders. We led them out into the prison courtyard and lined them up. The governor told them they were all to be killed." The captain paused.

Scarcely breathing, the missionary urged, "What happened next?"

The captain replied: "The strangest sight I have ever witnessed. Husbands and wives turned and kissed one another. The parents, smiling, spoke to their children of

'Yesu,' and pointed toward Heaven. There was no fear.

"They faced their executioners and began singing. And singing they died.

"When I saw how they faced death," the captain continued, "I knew that this 'Yesu' of whom they spoke truly must be God.

"Can God forgive my so-great sin? Is there nothing I might do to atone for my wrong?"

The missionary thought of his close friend who had been among those killed, and he reached for his worn Chinese Bible.

"Our God, whom we serve, is a merciful God. Your sin is great. But God's mercy is greater. This Jesus is His Son. He came to earth to die for sinners like you. I, too, am a sinner. Because Jesus died for you, God can forgive you."

The captain listened closely. Strange words these, to a mind schooled to hate, to kill: "Love ... Forgive ... Life." What he understood, he accepted.

It was late when the missionary escorted the captain to the gate. For a long time the missionary sat thinking. Fresh in his mind were hundreds of new graves strewn across China.

But no more asking the anguished, "Lord, why this great waste?"

The harvest had begun.

Prayer for the Day:

Dear God, You know the end from the beginning. In the midst of great tragedy, You turn hearts to You. Help me to share Your mercy even with those who may seem to me unforgivable.

Day 24

Do you not know that in a race all the runners run, but only one gets the prize? Run in such a way as to get the prize. Everyone who competes in the games goes into strict training. They do it to get a crown that will not last, but we do it to get a crown that will last forever. —1 CORINTHIANS 9:24–25

Just One Cheer?

I have often wondered why basketball has not made a tremendous hit in England. Due to the weather, one would think it would be an ideal sport. But from what we have heard, there is little or no place for an audience to sit, and no enthusiasm has been engendered for this particular sport. It makes one wonder how important it is for players to hear the reaction of the crowd.

"Wherefore seeing we also are compassed about with so great a cloud of witnesses, let us lay aside every weight, and the sin which doth so easily beset us, and let us run with patience the race that is set before us, looking unto Jesus the author and finisher of our faith" (Hebrews 12:1–2, KJV).

These verses are preceded by the great roll call of faith in Hebrews 11. And the picture I get is of a great stadium in which are seated all the saints who have preceded us, watching our progress. And I know that there are times in my own life when I have thought, "If only I could hear one cheer!"

———

Prayer for the Day:

Jesus, be with me today as I seek to stay on the course You have set before me. Even though I cannot hear the cheers of the saints, make me sensitive to Your approval.

Day 25

These were all commended for their faith, yet none of them received what had been promised, since God had planned something better for us so that only together with us would they be made perfect. —HEBREWS 11:39–40

Giants Among Us

Happy Christians were a part of my heritage. And those I knew were deeply committed to Christ. One would have to be to go to China in those days, learn the difficult language and work as hard as they did, often under dangerous circumstances.

For example, an oil company was about to open a new operation in China. A committee was charged with finding a man to manage the new division. This manager had to meet four qualifications: He had to be under 30 years of age, a university graduate, a proven leader and have a fluent knowledge of Chinese. Each man considered was found lacking.

Then someone said that they had a friend meeting all the requirements who already was living in the very city where the company was planning to establish its headquarters.

He was 28, had a brilliant college record, had three years' study and practice in the Chinese language, plus he had the full confidence of the Chinese people among whom he was well known. The committee asked how much salary this friend was getting and was startled to learn that it was only $600 a year because he worked for a mission board.

After further questioning, the committee chairman appointed the man to go to China and gave him the instructions, "Hire that man. Offer him $10,000 a year. If that fails, offer him $12,000 or even $15,000."

The man made the long trip, found his friend and made him the offer—which was declined. As instructed, the man raised the offer but was again refused.

Finally the man asked his friend, "What will you take?"

"It's not a question of the salary," the young missionary assured him. "The salary is tremendous. The trouble is with the job. The job is too little. I feel that God has called me to preach the Gospel of Christ. I should be a fool to quit preaching in order to sell oil."

Such were the giants among whom we grew up.

Prayer for the Day:

Lord, I am grateful for those around me who have been examples to me. I want to know and to do what You have called me to do with my life. Make me worthy as an example to others who come behind me.

Day 26

In him we have redemption through his blood, the forgiveness of sins, in accordance with the riches of God's grace.
—EPHESIANS 1:7

A Saintly Old Soul

Wang Nai Nai was our *amah* as we grew up, our Chinese nurse. We children loved her—everyone did. And with good reason: She loved everyone. I can still see her sitting on a low stool in the upstairs back bedroom, her paper hand-bound Chinese hymnal open in her hands, singing in her plain, flatly nasal voice the Chinese words to William Cowper's famous old hymn:

> There is a fountain filled with blood
> Drawn from Immanuel's veins,
> And sinners plunged beneath that flood
> Lose all their guilty stains.

And to my innocent child's mind, she was the picture of a saintly old soul at worship. Not until years later, when we were considered "old enough to be told about such things," did we learn how perfectly Cowper's old hymn fit her. When much younger, Wang Nai Nai and her husband had been "procurers." Baby girls generally were not wanted, so the shady business of buying them to sell to certain houses in Shanghai was not difficult.

But one day, "Aunt" Sophie Graham, one of the pioneer Presbyterian missionaries, told Wang Nai Nai about a God who loved her but hated sin. To become a child of God, one must repent of sin and ask God for forgiveness through His Son, Jesus. It was as blunt and simple as that.

Wang Nai Nai repented and turned to God.

Mother and Daddy told how when she first came to work for them, she longed to be able to read her Chinese Bible for herself. They found her flat on the floor one night, close to the fireplace with her Bible open, trying to learn the characters by the light of the dying fire. We had no electricity then, so they bought her a lamp of her own, and she taught herself to read the Bible.

Of such material God makes some of His choicest saints.

———❦———

Prayer for the Day:

Give me that same hunger, dear God, for Your Word that this dear saint had. I praise You for cleansing me from the stains of my sins. Show me how to live in such a way that others will see Your forgiveness and love.

Day 27

I will give you hidden treasures, riches stored in secret places, so that you may know that I am the Lord, the God of Israel, who summons you by name. —ISAIAH 45:3

A Crisis of Faith

When my parents sent me out of China to attend Pyeng Yang Foreign School in what is now North Korea, I had what some might call a crisis of faith, although that sounds a bit grand for a 13-year-old's first doubts. Perhaps the crisis resulted from what seemed like unanswered prayer. I had begged God (and my parents) to let me go home—without success. Or it might have been spiritual growing pains, like that of a young man who went to a delightfully sane bishop to confess he had lost his faith.

"Nonsense," replied the bishop. "You've lost your parents' faith. Now go out and get one of your own."

I knew that God had sent Jesus to die for mankind's sins, but somehow I did not feel included. There were so many people in the world and I was only one, and, let's face it, not a very significant one at that. I prayed for forgiveness and felt nothing. I wasn't even sure He was listening.

Finally, in desperation, I went to my ever-practical sister, Rosa, and asked her advice.

"I don't know what to tell you to do," she replied matter-of-factly, "unless you take some verse and put your own name in. See if that helps."

So I picked up my Bible and turned to Isaiah 53, one of my favorite chapters. I did just what she suggested. I read, *"He was wounded for [Ruth's] transgressions, he was bruised for [Ruth's] iniquities: the chastisement of [Ruth's] peace was upon him; and with his stripes [Ruth is] healed"* (Isaiah 53:5, KJV).

I knew then that I was included.

Prayer for the Day:

When I doubt Your faithfulness, Heavenly Father, help my unbelief. Remind me that You know my name and show me through Your Word that I am included in all Your promises.

Day 28

*Keep your lives free from the love of money and be content with what you have, because God has said, "Never will I leave you; never will I forsake you." —*HEBREWS 13:5

Promises

Among the most reassuring promises of Scripture are the I-am-with-you promises. They begin in Genesis where God says to Isaac, *"Fear not, for I am with thee"* (Genesis 26:24, KJV). They reach a glorious climax in Matthew 1:23, *"And they shall call his name Emmanuel, which being interpreted is, God with us"* (KJV).

Once again at the close of Matthew, as the risen Lord prepares to return to Heaven, He leaves His disciples with the promise, *"Lo, I am with you always"* (Matthew 28:20, KJV).

Our lives will be even happier as we bear in mind the words of the writer to the Hebrews, *"Let your conversation be without covetousness; and be content with such things as ye have: for he hath said, I will never leave thee, nor forsake thee"* (Hebrews 13:5, KJV). Having so great a Gift places all lesser gifts in proper perspective.

And all of time is marching toward that glorious fulfillment when, as He said, *"I will come again, and receive you unto myself; that where I am, there ye may be also"* (John 14:3, KJV).

He with us here—we with Him there. Emmanuel!

Prayer for the Day:

Jesus, You promised to be with me always. I claim that promise for today, and I ask You to help me be content. I look forward to the glorious day when all Your promises are completely fulfilled.

Day 29

If you, then, though you are evil, know how to give good gifts to your children, how much more will your Father in heaven give good gifts to those who ask him! —MATTHEW 7:11

Interrupted Plans

When I was in England with Bill for a Crusade, I wanted so much to get a copy of *Foxe's Book of Martyrs*. I had looked in some secondhand bookstores but with no success.

One day I was heading out of the hotel when a reporter asked if I could spend a few minutes with her. I was in a hurry, but I did the interview.

During the discussion, we talked about books that I had read, including Foxe's book. She mentioned that information in her article, and a woman who read the article called me and said that she had a very old copy available.

God used my love for books to teach me a lesson—that sometimes God interrupts our plans to accomplish His plans. I didn't think, when I was looking for those books in the secondhand bookstore, that God had something much better for me.

He leads every step of the way.

◆

Prayer for the Day:

Help me, Lord, to see interruptions in my day as opportunities for You to work in my life. When my own plans do not work out as I hoped, I will trust that You have something better planned for me. Give me the patience to wait for Your will to be accomplished.

Day 30

This is the confidence we have in approaching God: that if we ask anything according to his will, he hears us. —1 JOHN 5:14

Small Prayers?

"And please pray I'll catch a lizard."

Alone in the kitchen, catching up on the mail, I came across this very serious request sent to our organization from a very serious 4-year-old supporter.

I laughed out loud.

Only the day before, I had been in Paris with Bill for Mission France. Much prayer had gone up all over France in behalf of those who might be unfulfilled spiritually and stifled materially.

And here was a small boy praying for a lizard.

And God, our Father, who so graciously answered prayer in France, cared also for the concern of one 4-year-old.

I wondered how God not only puts up with, but welcomes, our prayers, considering all He has on Him. Not once has He ever said, "Don't bother Me. Don't you see I'm busy?" And He so well could—with the world in its present condition.

But, no. Each person is special to Him who calls every star by name, who has the hairs of our heads numbered and who knows the number of grains of sand on the ocean shores.

So even a little boy's desire for a lizard would be duly noted. In fact, I imagine the angels themselves enjoyed that small request.

Prayer for the Day:

Thank You, Lord, that You hear my prayers, no matter how big or small the concern may be. I know that You care about every detail of my life, and I want to commit each day to You.

Day 31

"For my Father's will is that everyone who looks to the Son and believes in him shall have eternal life, and I will raise them up at the last day." —JOHN 6:40

Our Old Home

Thomas Wolfe once wrote, "You can't go home again." But we tried.

My two sisters, Rosa and Virginia, our brother Clayton, and I returned to our old home in China in May 1980.

I recalled those spiritual giants of my childhood, the missionaries who had worked alongside my mother and father: We visited Uncle Jimmy and Aunt Sophie's house (now a wholesale grocery outlet), the girls' school where Lucy Fletcher had tutored us, the hospital compound (now an industrial school). So familiar, so changed. Our old home was graciously emptied for our inspection. Behind the welcoming banner stood all that was left—a pathetic reminder of the home that was—like an old woman no longer loved or cared for.

We even located the Chinese house in which I was born. For me it was like a death and a resurrection. Sentimental feelings for the place, nurtured lovingly over the decades, died. But an unimpeachable source had informed me earlier that the church in China today is both larger and stronger than when the missionaries were forced to leave. I realized afresh that God's work is not in buildings but in transformed lives.

Buildings fall into decay and eventually disappear. The transformed life goes on forever.

~~

Prayer for the Day:

Father, I am grateful to know I have a home with You forever because of my faith in Your Son. Help me to keep an eternal perspective about this life.

Sources

Morning Song; Feeling Trapped; Power in Prayer; Offering Christ; Our Father Carries Us; Falling Flat on One's Face; "I Didn't Do It!"; Salvaged, and Restored; Incompatible?; When Our Instructor Speaks; Capstones, Not Compactors; Scaffolding; Clogged Pens; Do We Make People "Thirsty"?; Harvest From Tragedy; Just One Cheer?; Interrupted Plans; Small Prayers? —Adapted from *Legacy of a Packrat* by Ruth Bell Graham, ©1989 Thomas Nelson Inc., Nashville, Tennessee. Used by permission. All rights reserved.

It's Time to Pray; Promises —Adapted from "Growing in Prayer" by Ruth Bell Graham, ©1974 The Ruth Graham Literary Trust. Used by permission.

The One I Missed, ©1982 The Ruth Graham Literary Trust. Used by permission.

Pure Refreshment; God Had Another Idea; Collectibles; Afraid? Of What?; Asking God "Why?"; Giants Among Us; A Saintly Old Soul; A Crisis of Faith; Our Old Home —Adapted from *It's My Turn* by Ruth Bell Graham, ©1982 Thomas Nelson Inc., Nashville, Tennessee. Used by permission. All rights reserved.

Look to the Rock —Adapted from "Missing and Meeting" by Ruth Bell Graham, ©1982 The Ruth Graham Literary Trust. Used by permission.

Steps to Peace With God

STEP 1 God's Purpose: Peace and Life

*God loves you and wants you to experience
peace and life—abundant and eternal.*

THE BIBLE SAYS ...

"We have peace with God through our
Lord Jesus Christ."
Romans 5:1

*Since God planned
for us to have
peace and the
abundant life right
now, why are most
people not having
this experience?*

"For God so loved the world that
He gave His only begotten Son, that
whoever believes in Him should not
perish but have everlasting life."
John 3:16, NKJV

"I have come that they may have
life, and that they may have it more
abundantly." *John 10:10, NKJV*

STEP 2 Our Problem: Separation From God

God created us in His own image to have an abundant life. He did not make us as robots to automatically love and obey Him, but gave us a will and a freedom of choice.

We chose to disobey God and go our own willful way. We still make this choice today. This results in separation from God.

THE BIBLE SAYS ...

"For all have sinned and fall short of the glory of God."
Romans 3:23

"For the wages of sin is death, but the gift of God is eternal life in Christ Jesus our Lord." *Romans 6:23*

Our choice results in separation from God.

Our Attempts

Through the ages, individuals have tried in many ways to bridge this gap ... without success ...

THE BIBLE SAYS ...

"There is a way that appears to be right, but in the end it leads to death." *Proverbs 14:12*

"But your iniquities have separated you from your God; and your sins have hidden His face from you, so that He will not hear." *Isaiah 59:2, NKJV*

There is only one remedy for this problem of separation.

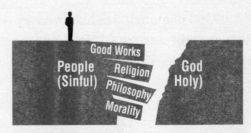

STEP 3   God's Remedy: The Cross

Jesus Christ is the only answer to this problem. He died on the cross and rose from the grave, paying the penalty for our sin and bridging the gap between God and people.

THE BIBLE SAYS ...

"For there is one God and one mediator between God and mankind, the man Christ Jesus." *1 Timothy 2:5*

"For Christ also suffered once for sins, the just for the unjust, that He might bring us to God." *1 Peter 3:18, NKJV*

"But God demonstrates his own love for us in this: While we were still sinners, Christ died for us." *Romans 5:8*

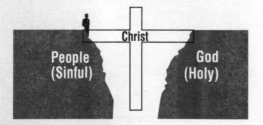

God has provided the only way ... we must make the choice ...

STEP 4 Our Response: Receive Christ

We must trust Jesus Christ and receive Him by personal invitation ...

THE BIBLE SAYS ...

"Behold, I stand at the door and knock. If anyone hears My voice and opens the door, I will come in to him and dine with him, and he with Me." *Revelation 3:20, NKJV*

"But as many as received Him, to them He gave the right to become children of God, to those who believe in His name." *John 1:12, NKJV*

"If you confess with your mouth the Lord Jesus and believe in your heart that God has raised Him from the dead, you will be saved." *Romans 10:9, NKJV*

Are you here ...   *or here?*

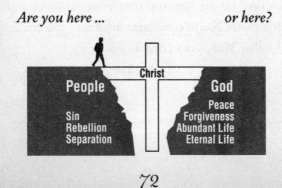

Is there any good reason why you cannot receive
Jesus Christ right now?

How to receive Christ:

1. Admit your need (I am a sinner).
2. Be willing to turn from your sins (repent).
3. Believe that Jesus Christ died for you on the cross and
   rose from the grave.
4. Through prayer, invite Jesus Christ to come in and control
   your life through the Holy Spirit. (Receive Him as Lord
   and Savior.)

What to Pray:

Dear Lord Jesus,

I know that I am a sinner, and I ask for Your forgiveness. I
believe You died for my sins and rose from the dead. I turn from
my sins and invite You to come into my heart and life. I want to
trust and follow You as my Lord and Savior.

In Your Name, Amen.

_____ _____

Date   Signature

God's Assurance: His Word

If you prayed this prayer,

THE BIBLE SAYS ...

"For 'whoever calls on the name of the Lord shall be saved.'" *Romans 10:13, NKJV*

Did you sincerely ask Jesus Christ to come into your life? Where is He right now? What has He given you?

"For it is by grace you have been saved, through faith—and this is not from yourselves, it is the gift of God—not by works, so that no one can boast." *Ephesians 2:8–9*

The Bible Says ...

"He who has the Son has life; he who does not have the Son of God does not have life. These things I have written to you who believe in the name of the Son of God, that you may know that you have eternal life, and that you may continue to believe in the name of the Son of God." *1 John 5:12–13, NKJV*

Receiving Christ, we are born into God's family through the supernatural work of the Holy Spirit who indwells every believer. This is called regeneration or the "new birth."

This is just the beginning of a wonderful new life in Christ. To deepen this relationship, you should:

1. Read your Bible every day to know Christ better.
2. Talk to God in prayer every day.
3. Tell others about Christ.
4. Worship, fellowship and serve with other Christians in a church where Christ is preached.
5. As Christ's representative in a needy world, demonstrate your new life by your love and concern for others.

God bless you as you do.
Billy Graham

If you are committing your life to Christ, please let us know!

We would like to send you Bible study materials to help you grow in your faith.

The Billy Graham Evangelistic Association exists to support and extend the evangelistic calling and ministries of Billy Graham and Franklin Graham by proclaiming the Gospel of the Lord Jesus Christ to all we can by every effective means available to us and by equipping others to do the same.

Our desire is to introduce as many people as we can to the person of Jesus Christ, so that they might experience His love and forgiveness.

Your prayers are the most important way to support us in this ministry. We are grateful for the dedicated prayer support we receive. We are also grateful for those who support us with financial contributions.

Billy Graham Evangelistic Association
1 Billy Graham Parkway
Charlotte, North Carolina 28201-0001
billygraham.org
Toll-free: 1-877-2GRAHAM
(1-877-247-2426)

Billy Graham Evangelistic Association of Canada
20 Hopewell Way NE
Calgary, Alberta T3J 5H5
billygraham.ca
Toll-free: 1-888-393-0003